Reaganomics
In Plain and Simple English

A BookCaps™ Study Guide
www.bookcaps.com

© 2012. All Rights Reserved.

Table of Contents

Introduction

At its most simple definition, Reaganomics is the term given the to the economic plan proposed and implemented by Ronald Reagan, the 40th president of the United States. However, the vast majority of historians agree that Reagan's economic policies had wide-reaching effects on American politics and society well after he left office in 1989. His plan and accompanying policies continue to draw both praise and criticism well into the 21st century.

Chapter 1: Why Reaganomics? The Word's Origin and Why Reagan Said the U.S. Needed It

American radio personality Paul Harvey is credited with coining the term "Reaganomics." Harvey was extremely popular and his folksy style of delivering news and his signature "Rest of the Story" verbal essays endeared him to millions. Unlike some who say it with a roll of their eyes, Harvey meant no disrespect to Reagan with the term "Reaganomics." In fact, Harvey viewed Reagan as something akin to the nation's savior. In 1981, Harvey wrote in his syndicated newspaper column that Reagan was delivering on his promises and that the "impeccable First Family" – which Americans later learned had its share of dysfunction - had restored dignity to the White House. Like Reagan, Harvey believed that the United States is "exceptional." President Reagan declared that America is "a land of hope, a light unto nations, a shining city on a hill." Writing in his memoirs, Harvey longed for this attitude among American leadership, well after Reagan left office.

The word "Reaganomics" was used before Reagan ever took office. During the 1980 presidential campaign, Reagan's main opponent in the Republican primaries was George Bush, Sr. As candidates often do, Bush seized the opportunity to mock Reagan's plan and famously called it "voo doo economics," expressing serious doubt that the plan would help fix the problems with the American economy. Bush may have regretted the statement when he was eventually selected to be Reagan's running mate and served as his vice-president for eight years. The country would later learn that some of Bush's concerns were valid.

What problems existed in the American economy? Plenty. The state of the economy was the central focal point of the 1980 election. The incumbent president, Democrat Jimmy Carter, had overseen one of the most disastrous economic periods in American history and Reagan ran on a platform of economic reform. He not only promised to fix the economy, he promised to fix it quickly and painlessly.

The United States faced a combination of rising unemployment and rising inflation that is known as stagflation – a stagnating economy and rising prices. When an economy is in a period of stagflation, prices for basic necessities, such as food, fuel and health care rise, which is the inflation part of the equation. However, incomes do not rise and allow consumers to keep up with costs. Businesses may close and unemployment likely rises – the economy is stagnating, or not growing.

There were multiple reasons that the U.S. was stuck in a period of stagflation. The Organization of Petroleum Exporting Companies (OPEC) issued an oil embargo in 1973. OPEC viewed this as punishment to the U.S. and other Western nations that had supported Israel. Oil supplies were cut and prices quadrupled. Gas cost approximately 25 cents a gallon in 1973. In a matter of months, the price shot up to $1 per gallon. The gas shortage was so severe that many gas stations limited sales. Lines to get up to a pump were often so long that there was an overflow of cars into the streets, while other stations simply ran out of gas.

Another reason for stagflation was that the U.S. was no longer the exporter of goods that it had been decades earlier. Concerns about "buying American" were very prevalent in the 1970s because more and more Americans were buying goods made elsewhere. That meant that fewer jobs were available in manufacturing and the U.S. was making less money selling those goods to other countries. A prime example is America's love for electronics. In the 1970s, many Americans wanted the latest gadgets such as videocassette recorders (VCRs) and portable tape players. By the end of the decade, more than half of the electronics that Americans purchased came from Asia. In the global market, West Germany began to produce more products in the metalwork machinery sector than the U.S. and even at home, a quarter of the American market for these goods went to foreign companies.

However, the biggest blow to American manufacturing was in the auto industry. The car was invented in the U.S. and was viewed as a truly American product. Losing its grip on the auto industry was devastating to the nation's manufacturing industry. The early signs were present as smaller, more economical cars began to become popular in California, but American car manufacturers did not recognize the danger that faced them when Toyota, Datsun (which later became Nissan), and Honda made better products that cost less. Lee Iacocca, the president of Chrysler Corporation, later said that the quality of Chrysler products was so poor at one point, the dealers expected to have to rebuild the cars when they arrived.

Arguably, one of the biggest overall contributors to stagflation was the decrease in productivity of American workers. This does not suggest that Americans were not working hard, but they were not as productive as they had been in previous years. Fewer goods were being produced. Americans were still the most productive workers in the world, but the rest of the world was catching up to the American rate of productivity per hour. There is no single theory as to why, but some economists believe that the influx of less experienced baby boomers and females into the work force played a role, as did the cost of having to comply with government environmental, safety and health regulations.

Chapter 2: The 1980 Election

Because the final tally of electoral votes heavily favored Reagan, it is often stated that Reagan defeated Carter in a "landslide." While that is accurate – Reagan took a whopping 489 electoral votes to Carter's 49 – the race to the White House was much closer than that. Despite the concerns about the economy, there were bigger concerns about whether or not Reagan was up to the job. Some thought he might be too old. Just shy of his 70th birthday, he was- and still is - the oldest person to assume the office of the president. There were also those who were uncertain that Reagan had the political skill needed and a sound grasp of the issues. This was despite the fact that Reagan had served as governor of California, which is not only the largest state in the union, but is larger than most countries. To many potential voters, though, the former movie star was simply an aging actor.

Going into the final week of the election, Carter and Reagan were running neck-and-neck. Journalist Elizabeth Drew, the author of "Portrait of an Election: The 1980 Presidential Campaign," said that on the final Friday before the election, it was for all intents and purposes, "a tie." Carter had been pushing for a debate, presumably to show that he was better suited to guide the country out of its problems than Reagan. Carter's campaign hoped that Reagan would slip up during the debate and appear less equipped than Carter to right the country's wrongs. After much resistance, Reagan finally agreed to the late-October debate because the race was so close and his camp believed he needed a final push before Election Day. The result was a major turning point for Reagan, who asked potential voters, "Are you better off than you were four years ago?" If not, he suggested that they had an alternative – they could vote for him.

The question struck a chord with most of the voters because many were not better off than they had been four years ago. Prices were high and rising, jobs were scarce and they were weary of the country's malaise, a term that became associated with Carter even though he never used that word. When Reagan promised a plan that would put more money in their pockets, Americans were ready to listen.

Chapter 3: The Policies of Reaganomics

If the American people were ready to listen to Reagan, it is not necessarily true that the House of Representatives was. When Reagan took office in January 1981, as was the case throughout both of his terms, the Democrats controlled the House. Speaker of the House Tip O'Neill said of the Republicans, "We're not going to let them tear asunder programs we've built over the years." However, the Republicans did have control of the Senate and conservative Democrats in the House were good at getting liberals to see things their way. Then, a near-tragedy on March 30, 1981 may have helped swing support of the majority of the nation in Reagan's favor.

In an effort to win the attention of actress Jodie Foster, John Hinckley, Jr. shot President Reagan as he was leaving the Hilton Hotel in Washington, D.C., barely two months after he began his first term. Three other men were wounded, including Reagan's press secretary, James Brady. The Secret Service was not sure how badly he was wounded until he began to spit up bright red blood in the back of the presidential limousine. A bullet had punctured Reagan's lung. Miraculously, the bullet malfunctioned and failed to explode on impact. It rested an inch from his heart. Most Americans were unaware just how severe the injury was.

Reagan's humor through the crisis, famously telling his wife, Nancy, "Honey, I forgot to duck," and his apparent quick recovery endeared him to the nation. It is now known that Reagan's recovery was much more difficult, but this was kept from the American public, as was information about how close Reagan came to death. Regardless, the failed assassination attempt leaves some debate about how it may have impacted the Democrats and their initial willingness to challenge a man whose courage during his near-death experience inspired the country.

Four Primary Objectives of Reaganomics

Reaganomics can be boiled down to four primary economic objectives:

1.) Reduce tax rates to put more money in the pockets of American consumers.
2.) Reduce government spending.
3.) Support the Federal Reserve's plan to tighten the availability of money to combat inflation.
4.) Deregulation, with the hope that there will be reduced costs for consumers and businesses.

Reaganomics Tax Policies

The heart of Reaganomics is a theory called supply-side economics. The basis of supply-side economics is increasing revenue, or the money the government takes in, by decreasing taxes, which is the money people pay to the government. While it may seem counterintuitive, Reagan and his financial advisors believed that if taxes were cut, Americans would have more money to spend and invest. If Americans invested and spent more money, Reagan believed that the government would bring in more revenue.

Reagan was actually taking a page from theories of new economists like Jude Wanniski and George Gilder, who morphed the economic theories of John Maynard Keyes into supply-side economics. Keynesian theory is quite different, arguing that consumer demand for goods and services are key to the economy and if demand falls, that will drag the economy into a recession. Supply-siders believe that producers of goods and services are more important and the more they are created, the more the economy will grow. In 1979 New York's Representative Jack Kemp and Delaware's Senator William Roth developed what became to be known as the Kemp-Roth Bill. It proposed a 30 percent cut in federal income taxes and provided the basis for the focal point of Reaganomics.

Some of Reagan's motivation for pushing for large-scale tax cuts was rooted in his own personal experience. At the height of his acting career with Warner Brothers, he was in the 94 percent marginal tax bracket. He was paying so much in taxes, he wondered if working was even worth it, but realized if he didn't work, other lower-paid staff that worked on his films would not get paid at all. This type of thinking is an example of "trickle-down economics," which is a theory that claims tax breaks and incentives for the wealthy will provide more opportunity for the poor, improving the economy as a whole.

Chapter 4: Economic Recovery Tax Act of 1981

The Economic Recovery Tax Act of 1981 (ERTA) was passed in August. It amounted to a $750 billion tax cut over 5 years, the largest in US history. One of the key elements is that it lowered the top marginal income tax rate from 70 percent to 50 percent. Marginal tax rate is very different from the effective tax rate. It refers to the tax rate on the last dollar earned. For example, if a single taxpayer makes $100,000 per year and, based on the chart provided by the Internal Revenue Service (IRS) that person falls into the 28 percent tax bracket, this does not mean that the taxpayer is taxed at a flat rate of 28 percent. The amount of tax is not $28,000. Only part of the $100,000 income is taxed at 28 percent. As the taxpayer climbs higher in the tax bracket, the last dollars earned are taxed at a higher rate.

Going back to Reagan's concern about taxes when he was making movies for Warner Brothers and the marginal tax rate was 94 percent, once Reagan reached the upper echelon of taxable income, he pocketed very little of the money he earned. At one point, he pocketed only 6 percent of his pay. As Reagan pointed out, he had very little incentive to make a movie at that point, other than considering the effect it would have had on other people if he stopped making those movies. Reducing the marginal income rate to 50 percent in 1981 theoretically provided a greater incentive to keep working and keep producing.

Reagan also phased in a 23 percent reduction in personal income taxes over the next three years. This was across the board, meaning that it did not matter if the taxpayer was rich, poor, or somewhere in between; the overall 23 percent reduction applied. The act also called for tax brackets to be adjusted for inflation beginning in 1984. Without this provision, taxpayers were subject to "bracket creep." This was a problem for the American economy in the late 1970s and into the early 1980s because inflation caused incomes to rise, which pushed some taxpayers into a higher tax bracket, but prices for goods and services are so high that those taxpayers did not really have more spending power.

Businesses also received tax breaks courtesy of ERTA. Depreciation guidelines were more liberal, making it easier for businesses to write off assets, the business investment tax credit was increased, and there were deep cuts in business, gift, and estate taxes.

Tax Equity and Fiscal Responsibility Act (TEFRA)

In response to a growing budget deficit, the 1982 Tax Equity and Fiscal Responsibility Act (TEFRA) scaled back some of the tax cuts from ERTA the previous year and Reagan hoped it would help generate more revenue. Signed in September, TEFRA removed some of the tax breaks, such as how a business could claim depreciation of assets. It temporarily raised taxes on cigarettes and telephone service. Penalties for failure to pay income taxes were increased and it was more difficult to claim medical deductions.

Tax Reform Act of 1986

The 1986 tax reform was not an easy sell, even to Reagan's fellow Republicans. It took two years of campaigning and he was only able to get the act passed after making a personal visit to Capitol Hill to make his case for the bill. The effect of this act was to relieve millions of low-income families from paying income tax, as well as moving a large share of the tax burden from individuals to corporations. He stated that his motivation was to close tax loopholes and make sure that they wealthiest Americans paid their fair share of taxes, despite the pleas of these taxpayers, many of whom were ardent Reagan supporters.

The 1986 reform bill also further reduced the to marginal income tax rate, this time to 28 percent. Tax code provisions such as the investment tax credit, which primarily benefits industries such as railroads or utilities were eliminated. "Idea-based" industries, such as software companies, had their corporate tax rates reduced. In 1986, the year after the law went into effect, the tax rates for Oracle and Microsoft both went down over 10%.

Chapter 5: Reaganomics and Inflation

Inflation is the rate at which the price for goods and services rise. If inflation gets too high, purchasing power is decreased. For example, if inflation is 5 percent, then a one-dollar soft drink will cost $1.05. Inflation is determined by the consumer price index, which gives the average cost of consumer goods and services, including health care, for urban consumers. In 1979, the inflation stood at nearly 14 percent, prompting potential voters in the 1980 presidential election to rank inflation as a problem three times more important than unemployment, which was also high, hovering over 7 percent.

Reagan promised a quick end to inflation. In order to fight the rising prices that were gripping the nation, Federal Reserve Board Chairman Paul Volcker raised interest rates, meaning borrowing money was going to cost more. As a result, the consumer demand for money was not equal to the money available and spending ground to a halt. As spending slowed, prices came down and so did inflation. Inflation dropped nine points over the first three years of the Reagan administration. Reagan's goal of whipping inflation was achieved, but there would be a cost.

Inflation from 1979 - 1983

1979 – 13.3%
1980 – 12.4%
1981 – 8.9%
1982 – 3.9%
1983 – 3.8%

Chapter 6: Reaganomics and Government Spending

Make no mistake, Reagan hated big government. He made that point clear before he even set foot in his new office, when he said in his inaugural address in 1981, "Government is not the solution to our problem; government **is** our problem." He made it one of his main goals to cut back on the amount of money the federal government was spending. Social programs were his primary target.

"The Reagan Diaries," published in 2007, gives tremendous insight into why Reagan made some of the decisions he made. Reagan kept a handwritten diary of his thoughts and activities nearly every day he spent as president. Some entries were as simple as what football game he watched that day. However, he also made his view on government-funded social programs very clear. While some argued that Reagan was attacking Franklin Delano Roosevelt's "New Deal" – and Reagan was quick to point out that he voted for FDR four times back when he was still a Democrat – Reagan was really going after Lyndon Johnson's "Great Society."

The main focus of the Great Society was civil rights and poverty, but LBJ also ushered in an avalanche of programs for the environment, the arts, education, and health care. Programs, laws, and terms that are now part of American culture such as the Civil Rights Acts of 1964 and 1968, Medicare, Medicaid, Head Start, and even Sesame Street, thanks to funding for the Public Broadcasting System, exist because of the Great Society. Johnson, who tried to pay for both the Great Society and the Vietnam War without raising taxes, famously declared a war on poverty in 1964. Reagan wrote in his diary that it was this war on poverty that led the country "into this mess." He believed that spending on social programs could go on indefinitely, if allowed to, and he was intent on putting on the brakes.

Even Reagan's critics admit that he had a way with words. He was not called "the Great Communicator" for nothing and certainly, his training as an actor helped him tell a story. One story he repeatedly told was one of a "welfare queen" from Chicago. This liar and cheat supposedly drove a Cadillac to pick up her welfare checks, which she got by using 80 aliases, 30 addresses, and multiple social security cards to defraud the government of over $150,000. Journalists anxious to interview this woman were never able to verify her existence.

Going back even further, as the host of the 1950s and 1960s television program, "General Electric Theater," Reagan also served as a company spokesman. He regularly spoke about the waste of big government. He referred to the bankruptcy of the "welfare state" and called for a drastic reduction in the government. General Electric, which had millions of dollars worth of contracts and could not afford political controversy, fired Reagan in 1962 when he said that the federally owned Tennessee Valley Authority, which provides power to states in the southern U.S., was part of the problem with government.

The word "welfare" can be very powerful and Reagan used it to his advantage. Neither Democrats nor Republicans want to shell out taxes to pay for welfare for people too lazy to find work. In 1992, CBS News and "The New York Times" conducted a survey about the word "welfare." The survey showed that 44 percent of people polled felt that the government was spending too much money on "welfare." However, when asked about government spending on "assistance to the poor," only 13 percent thought there was too much spending and 64 percent thought the government should spend more.

In the first budget that Reagan presented to Congress for its approval in February 1981, it contained $45 billion in spending cuts. The budget that was passed in August approved $35 billion in cuts. The Democratic chairman of the House Budget Committee, James Jones of Oklahoma, said the cuts were "the most monumental and historic turnaround in fiscal policy that has ever occurred."

Reagan tried unsuccessfully to eliminate federal housing, although he did cut the spending on low-income housing in half, to $17.5 billion, in his first year in office. The overall number of eligible poor receiving federal subsidies declined in the 1980s and by the middle of the decade, over 8.9 million renter households existed for the available 5.6 million low-cost housing units. This left 3.3 million people unable to secure low-income housing.

Reagan also targeted the Aid to Families with Dependent Children (AFDC) program, which provides income assistance to eligible low-income families. The 1981 budget placed new restrictions on income eligibility and, by increasing the amount awarded on an individual basis, decreased the number of recipients. School lunch programs were also reduced.

He was warned by advisors not to try to cut Social Security and Medicare, although Regan did reduce aid to people with disabilities. In 1985, Reagan set his sights on slashing higher education spending on those looking for financial assistance in attending college. Among his proposals to Congress was the elimination of federal student financial aid to families with an adjusted gross income over $32,500. Students whose families made over $25,000 per year were to be denied work study jobs and grants, and federal aid was to be capped at $4,000 per year.

This set off a storm of controversy among those in higher education, who did not want the budget deficit to be cut at the expense of students in need of aid. The cuts would have totaled $2.3 billion. Reagan also proposed slashing spending on National Institutes of Health funding, a major source of funding for science-based research for universities. Rallies, protests and campaigns against the proposed cuts reverberated across the nation. Massachusetts Senator John Kerry pointed out that the cost of Reagan's "Star Wars" missile defense program would cover the entire financial aid program. The measure did not pass.

When Reagan vowed to reduce the size of government, this did not include national defense and Star Wars was a major recipient of funds. He believed in what he called "peace by strength." As much as Reagan hated big government, he also hated Communism. This was another deep-rooted belief held by Reagan, dating back to the Red Scare of the 1950s. He was cooperative in the effort to rid Hollywood of Communism at a time when many in the entertainment industry were wrongly accused of having Communist beliefs. Reagan said that the attempts by the Communists to take over the movie business was what changed his own political beliefs from Democrat to Republican.

In a 1982 speech to the British House of Commons, Reagan referred to the Soviet Union as the "evil empire" and then said it again in a speech to the National Association of Evangelicals in 1983. Reagan drew the term from the blockbuster movie, "Star Wars." He was convinced that the U.S. needed to be prepared for military intervention to prevent the Soviet Union from spreading Communism into Western Europe and Third World countries, as well as to prevent a Soviet missile attack on the U.S. He proposed the Star Wars program in 1983, which was intended to include a space-based missile defense system and an earthbound laser battle stations that would detect Soviet missiles and shoot them out of the sky. Since Reagan proposed the program, the U.S. has spent over $100 billion on missile defense.

Star Wars was not the only high ticket item in Reagan's defense spending. The *Trident* submarine carried a $1.5 billion price tag. It could fire hundreds of nuclear warheads, but was only useful in the event of nuclear war. Critics argued that if called into action, the *Trident* would only add a few hundred weapons to the ten of thousands of nuclear war heads already at the U.S.'s disposal.

By 1987, the Reagan administration doubled the nation's defense spending, accounting for more than $330 billion of the budget. Even though this spending was justified in part by fears of a Soviet invasion of Western Europe, George Kennan, former ambassador to the Soviet Union, claimed that there was no basis for this fear. In the 1980s, Harry Rositzke, formerly the CIA director for espionage operations wrote, "In all of my years in government and since I have never seen an intelligence estimate that shows how it would be profitable to Soviet interests to invade Western Europe or to attack the United States."

Much of this defense spending was against the budget director's will. As David Stockman hovered over the budget and looked for budget cuts wherever they were available, defense seemed like a logical area because he thought some of that spending was wasteful. Not only that, but if the administration cut defense spending, it might make it easier to argue for cuts in other areas. However, Secretary of Defense Caspar Weinberger continued to overrule Stockman and when all was said in done, the Reagan administration had spent nearly $2 trillion in defense buildup.

Reaganomics and Deregulation

Although Reagan is often associated with deregulation, the process of loosening government regulations on industries had already begun. The Carter administration oversaw the deregulation of the airlines in 1978, the railroads in 1976, and the trucking industry in 1980. Still, many in the Reagan administration portrayed the country as drowning in red tape. In 1981, Reagan appointed Vice-President Bush as the head of a task force to review all federal agencies and regulations, looking for areas to cut spending and promote competition. By 1983, the Bush task force had reviewed 119 regulations. 76 of those were revised or eliminated completely. By this time, Reagan had also signed Executive Order 12291, which said that before a government agency could propose new regulations, that agency needed to show cost versus benefit.

Rather than having the government set prices, deregulation counts on the market and competition between private companies to set prices. This does not always happen exactly as planned, though, as deregulating the airlines proved. Before deregulation, the government determined airfares, which airlines could offer commercial flights, and what routes the airlines could fly. After deregulation, many prices for flights that were not between major hubs skyrocketed. On the other hand, deregulation was successful in reducing airfare for flights between big cities.

Reagan oversaw the conclusion of the dismantling of the largest public utility in the country, which helped set the stage for deregulation in the communication industry. In 1970, American Telephone and Telegraph (AT&T) was the world's largest company. It had $53 billion in assets and had a monopoly on the telecommunications industry because government regulations prevented other companies from entering the market. It provided all local telephone service through the Bell System, nearly all long-distance phone calls, and provided virtually all of the equipment needed to provide the U.S. with telephone service. When Americans referred to the term "Ma Bell," they were referring to the telephone system.

In 1969, the government allowed the MCI Corporation to compete with AT&T for long distance customers. This led to even more competitors trying to enter the market and, in 1974 the U.S. Department of Justice brought an anti-trust lawsuit against AT&T. The suit accused AT&T of being a monopoly, which is illegal in the United States. The lawsuit was finally settled in 1981 and AT&T was split into seven regional holding companies in 1984, which were known as Baby Bells. Interestingly, Reagan was personally opposed to breaking up AT&T, believing that it was a national treasure. However, he was assured by Assistant Attorney General for Antitrust William Baxter that the only way to encourage competition for long distance phone service was to break up AT&T.

Old regulatory rules imposed on the Federal Communications Commission (FCC) were eliminated by the Reagan administration. The FCC is an independent government agency that regulates television, radio, satellite, cable, and wire communications. It is funded entirely by regulatory fees paid by licensed providers of communications. The FCC is often viewed as the watchdog for communications. For example, it is the FCC that levies fines for radio personalities or television programs that overstep boundaries with obscenity or profanity. Prior to deregulation the FCC had a rule called the "fairness doctrine." It dated back to before the FCC even existed, in 1939, and said that broadcast licensees, such as radio stations, to provide equal airtime for opposing viewpoints on issues of public importance. The FCC stopped enforcing the rule in 1987 and it was officially scrapped in 2011.

Congress also oversaw the deregulation of the natural gas industry in 1985. Reagan also took aim at the Environmental Protection Agency (EPA). He felt that the cost of regulating pollution and air quality was too high. By 1984, the EPA's staff was cut by 29 percent and the total EPA budget was slashed by 44 percent. Among Reagan's infamous quotes about his stance on the environment were, "trees cause more pollution than automobiles do," and "if you've seen one tree, you've seen them all." Reagan's secretary of the interior, James Watt, earned no more of a reputation for being a friend to environmental causes than Reagan. Watt supported turning federal land over for oil drilling and mining and showed little interest in land conservation. He resigned in 1983 after saying that his advisory panel for coal-leasing in Wyoming was comprised of, "a black ... a woman, two Jews, and a cripple."

One of the biggest deregulation undertakings by the Reagan administration was the president's expansion on banking deregulation, which started under the Carter administration. Both Carter and Reagan believed that removing the majority of federal regulations on banks would help the banks be more profitable. The belief was that banks could make more money by competing on the open market and that consumers would benefit by having lower interest rates on borrowed money. The Depository Institutions Deregulation Act signed by President Carter in 1980 was intended to bring new deposits to savings and loans (S&Ls) by allowing them to set higher interest rates. People depositing money into S&Ls could also have federal protection up to $100,000 per account, rather than $40,000.

However, this did not take into account the fact that the S&Ls would pay more to the new depositors for interest on their accounts, while still having longer-term loans, like mortgages, paying them very low interest under the old rules. By 1981, 85 percent of S&Ls lost money. In 1982 Congress addressed the problem by passing the Garn - St. Germain Act. This bank deregulation program under Reagan presented many changes:

A. Maximum interest rates of savings accounts were eliminated. Banks were now free to set whatever interest rate they chose.
B. Any type of bank was permitted to offer a checking account.
C. All depository institutions could borrow money from the federal government in exchange for depositing a certain percentage of their money with the government. This used to only be permitted with commercial banks. The purpose was to help stabilize the banks.
D. Savings banks could now issue credit cards and offer commercial and non-residential real estate loans. This was previously only allowed with commercial banks.

Congress's attempt at a fix would result in one of the biggest scandals in American banking history.

Chapter 7: Outcome

Outcomes of Reaganomics

As much as the tax cuts sounded like a good idea to Americans, it resulted in less revenue for the government. Because there was less revenue, the U.S. was forced to borrow more and more money. The historic spending cuts in the 1981 budget may have felt victorious to the Reagan administration at the time, but David Stockman, director of the Office of Management and Budget, warned of trouble ahead. He said, "We're heading for a crash landing on the budget." And he was right.

The problem was that revenue was lagging worse than anticipated, but spending was still going up. Bringing in less money while spending more is a recipe for disaster for any budget, especially the federal government's. That meant the country was headed for a deficit of monumental proportions.

There were several reasons for the deficit. For one thing, the administration had just won a huge tax cut, one that was even bigger than first envisioned. It was not just that personal income tax was reduced, but the cuts in business, estate, and gift taxes took away revenue, too. The Reagan administration also predicted a balanced budget by 1984 (something that never occurred), which was the basis for the 1981 budget. Supply-side economics was not working as well or as fast as Reagan's advisors had hoped. Combine all of this with the fact that the Federal Reserve tightened the money supply by raising interest rates and that all equaled a major recession near the end of 1981 and throughout 1982.

On the plus side, inflation was being beat back by the raised interest rates, but even that worked against Reagan, at first. As inflation eased, there was less "bracket creep" and since fewer people were being pushed into higher tax brackets, the government was making less money. Some also argued, including Stockman, that as drastic as Reagan's cuts into spending on social programs were, they were not deep enough to help bridge the deficit gap. Stockman said that Reagan was "too kind, gentle, and sentimental," to make those kind of cuts and even Stockman admitted that the type of budget slashing he was personally hoping for would have "hurt millions of people in the short run."

As the country slid deeper and deeper into financial problems, Reagan wrote in his diary, "We are really in trouble. We look at $200 billion in deficits if we can't pull of some miracles." Jobs were lost at a level not seen since the Great Depression, farmers lost their property to foreclosure, millions became homeless, and businesses went under. By the end of Reagan's second year, Stockman declared the country's money situation to be "an utter, mind-numbing catastrophe."

The country did recover, but the final outcome of Reagan's performance with the budget was as bad as any president who had ever served. In each one of his eight years in office, the country spent more money than it brought in. The smallest deficit was in fiscal 1982, the year of the great recession, when the U.S. was $127.9 billion in the red. The largest deficit was in fiscal 1986, when the deficit soared to over $221 billion. By the time he left office, President Reagan oversaw an administration that tripled the nation's debt, from $914 billion in fiscal 1980 to $2.7 trillion in 1989. Dick Darman, the budget director for Bush, Sr., said that the Reagan administration added more debt to the federal budget than all of the other presidential administrations combined.

James M. Poterba, an economist from MIT, analyzed the budget and offered his reasons for the bloated deficit that became part of Reagan's legacy. He estimated that one-third of the growth in the deficit was due to Reagan's tax cuts and two-third due to increased spending, largely due to defense and interest payments on borrowed money. As the U.S. hemorrhaged money, the government was forced to stop working – even if briefly – 12 times on Reagan's watch. For presidents to come, Reagan left the budget as the nation's primary political concern.

Ironically, even with all of discourse about welfare and the cutting of program, spending on social welfare increased under the Reagan administration. The government spent $313 billion on social programs in 1980 and by 1988, it was spending $533 billion. Some of this was due to shifting where the government was spending. For example, even though funding for the AFDC program decreased by 1 percent, spending on the Earned Income Tax Credit for low-income workers actually doubled. Still, the reduction of the school lunch program left more than a million poor children without their one nutritious meal per day. Millions more were officially poor, living in families below the poverty line threshold of $900 per month. In most cases, state aid accounted for only $500 to $700 per month as the federal government also decreased funding to states and cities.

The message coming from the Reagan administration was that the wealth would "trickle down" to the nation's poor because of the tax cuts, but one mother responded to this assessment with a letter to her local newspaper. In the letter, she wrote:

> I am on Aid to Families with Dependent Children, and both my children are in school. ... I have graduated from college with distinction, 128th in a class of over 1000, with a B.A. in English and sociology. I have experience in library work, child care, social work and counseling.

I have been to the CETA office. They have nothing for me....
I also go every week to the library to scour the newspaper
Help Wanted ads. I have kept a copy of every cover letter
that I have sent out with my resume; the stack is inches thick.
I have applied for jobs paving as little as $8000 a year. I
work part-time in a library for $3.50 an hour, welfare reduces
my allotment to compensate. . ..

It appears we have employment offices that can't employ,
governments that can't govern and an economic system that
can't produce jobs for people ready to work.. . .

Another problem that boomed during the recession did not go away
and continued to plague Reagan throughout both terms was
homelessness. The gap between available subsidized housing and
those eligible left millions homeless well after Reagan left office. In
a December 23, 1988 interview with David Brinkley on ABC News,
Reagan denied that his administration was responsible for the
homelessness problem that surged in the 80s, and famously
commented that many "make it their own choice for staying out
there." He frequently said that many of the nation's homeless were
mentally impaired, released from institutions due to lawsuits by the
American Civil Liberties Union. The United States Conference of
Mayors partially agreed with this assessment, but also reported that
20 percent of the nation's homeless at that time were employed but
unable to afford housing.

Reagan was able to quickly – even if not painlessly – one of his goals, which was to curb inflation. He does not always receive credit for this because reducing inflation is not something that a president can do without the Federal Reserve, but the Federal Reserve does benefit from the president's support. Paul Volcker, the Federal Reserve Chairman, was appointed by Carter and Reagan was under a great deal of pressure to replace him. However, Reagan not only detested inflation, he understood that without stable prices of everyday goods, the economy could not recover and that Americans would continue to be afraid that prices would simply continue to spiral out of control.

Reagan did understand that if Volcker raised interest rates, it would lead to a recession. It was only logical that tightening a hold on the money would result in decreased spending. By December of 1980, the prime lending rate for the banks, which is the rate offered the most credit-worthy borrowers was 21.5 percent, which was an all-time high. By the following summer, many Americans could not afford to buy houses or cars. Companies could not grow because they could not borrow, and production plummeted. The auto industry suffered a 56 percent decrease in production and steel saw a 56 percent decline. By 1982, construction of new homes fell to 40 percent the 1979 level, and unemployment was at 10.8 percent, the highest it had been since World War II. As Reagan was raked over the coals in the media and his approval rating plummeted, he urged Volcker – and Americans – to stay the course. And by 1983, with inflation holding under 4 percent, Reagan had, indeed, slayed the inflation dragon.

The outcome of deregulation in the Reagan administration, as whole, was mixed. One of the most obvious deregulation successes was the breakup of AT&T and the deregulation of the telecommunications industry. This, along with Reagan's tax breaks for idea-based industries set the stage for the telecommunications boom of the 1990s. Virtually unknown when Reagan was elected in 1980, the internet began to appear in American households in the mid to late 1990s and a decade later, would become as commonplace as television. Many AT&T employees suffered personally through job loss or demotion, but the move benefited the country as a whole.

The scrapping of the fairness doctrine that went along with the deregulation of the communications industry has – for better or worse – opened the door for bipartisan news programs on radio and television. Fox News Network appeared on the scene in 1996 and unquestionably presents right-leaning views of American politics. MSNBC counters with left-leaning pundits. No matter which side Americans fall on, deregulation led to a proliferation of unmoderated political discussion on America's airwaves

If the Reagan administration is remembered for any single aspect of deregulation, it is banking. Banking deregulation was a financial disaster that led to one of the biggest banking scandals in American history. The Garn-St. Germain Act of 1982 allowed S&Ls to invest in areas that could allow them to be more profitable, such as business loans, junk bonds, and commercial real estate. S&Ls were now not any different than commercial banks and could just as easily invest in a new shopping mall or office complex.

Certainly these circumstances combined to create an environment that was very inviting to shysters and crooks looking to make a quick buck. Some S&Ls were purchased with the intent of defrauding investors. Highly speculative loans were increasingly becoming the norm. However, a big reason that this was allowed to happen in the first place is that the federal government also removed much of the federal oversight of S&Ls. As riskier loans were allowed, the accounting rules became more liberal and the number of bank examiners was reduced. For example, in Texas, which led the nation in S&L failures, had its number of regulators dropped from 54 to 12 between 1981 and 1985.

The Keating Five was led by Charles H. Keating, the head of California's Lincoln Savings and Loan Association. The group was made up of five senators: Alan Cranston of California, Dennis DeConcini of Arizona, John McCain of Arizona, John Glenn of Ohio, and Donald Riegle, Jr. of Michigan. When the federal government investigated the lending practices of Lincoln Savings and Loan, the Keating Five were accused of intervening with regulators on Keating's behalf. Over 23,000 bondholders and investors were defrauded, with many losing their life savings. Keating's S&L sold $250 million worth of bonds, which were later defaulted. His investors thought that their money was protected by the federal government, but it was not. The Lincoln S&L ultimately collapsed in 1989 and cost the federal government over $3 billion he Keating Five were publicly admonished by Congress, while Keating went to federal prison for five years on racketeering charges.

Reagan is not usually held responsible by historians for this historic collapse. There were far too many players to single him out. However, the collapse of the S&Ls did not occur overnight and it became evident that many of the institutions were either badly managed, bankrupt, or both. Many economists and historians believe that had the government acted more quickly in closing the so-called "zombie" instructions, as in the walking dead, the crisis may not have been as bad as it was. By allowing these institutions to continue to make bad loans well into the mid-1980s, more money was lost and wasted on operating expenses. In the end, half of the countries S&Ls went bankrupt.

Positive Interpretations of Reaganomics

Supporters of Reaganomics point out that despite some painful periods in his eight years in the White House, Reaganomics was a success and, overall, he stuck to his goals. Reagan led the U.S. out of the economic turmoil of 1970s into a decade of prosperity for millions of Americans. He not only restored the economy, he helped America regain its confidence. The tax cuts that were a central focus of Reaganomics increased the cash flow for millions of people. The economic boom of the 1980s saw the creation of new businesses, which in turn let to 19 million new jobs. Many Americans became very wealthy, with one marketing expert counting over 100,000 Americans with a net worth of over $10 million, which was more than the U.S's share of citizens worth just $1 million in the 1960s. The poorest Americans, with their mean income in the bottom 20 percent, saw their income rise 5 percent in the 1980s and half of the people who were at the bottom of the income scale were making more money by the end of the decade.

Even though it contributed to a major recession, Reagan kept his campaign promise of whipping inflation, which plummeted to less than 4 percent in his final two years in office. The low marginal tax rates helped stimulate the decade's economic growth and created a more favorable economy for lower income brackets. Eventually, the economy recovered and growth of the nation was evident in:

Investment - 51% growth

Production of industry – 30% growth

Manufacturing productivity – 26% growth

Per-capita income – 18% increase

Reagan also paved the way for telecommunications with his tax support for idea-based industries, allowing companies such as Microsoft to flourish. Continuing the policies of deregulation reduced red tape and government costs, while allowing the free market to set competitive prices for consumers. While the deficit did increase, the increase in defense spending was a crucial element to taking a stand against the Soviets. Rather than working toward not losing the Cold War, as previous presidents had done, Reagan helped ensure that the Cold War was over by the end of the decade.

Negative Interpretations of Reaganomics

Critics of Reagan's policies counter the argument that Reaganomics created more jobs, there is the point that the highest paying blue collar jobs went away with the manufacturing base. While new jobs may have been created, many of them were low-paying service jobs. Reagan also oversaw the largest increase in the federal deficit in history, which some historians claim may have helped his goal of reducing social programs by "starving" them. After all, if the country is for all intents and purposes out of money, it is the not the time to ask for new programs. Worse yet, Democrats would be forced to ask for tax increases to cover the programs, which is the last thing most politicians want to do.

Despite Reagan's platform of decreased spending, he spent billions on defense and by the time he left office, the country was $3 trillion in debt. While his strategic defense initiative likely did intimidate the Soviet Union, the Star Wars plan was based more on science fiction that actual science. There was no conceivable way it could be built, yet billions have spent trying. Reagan seemed unable to grasp the impossibility of this challenge and continued to pour dollars into a concept that nobody really understood. What's more, critics claim that Reagan actually prolonged the Cold War, rather than ended it. His continual posturing with the Soviets made it more difficult for Mikhail Gorbachev, the president of the USSR, to convince his own government that the U.S. could be trusted.

Perhaps the biggest criticism leveled at Reaganomics is that the rich got richer. The tax cuts that stimulated the economy increased the gap between the wealthy and the poor. The idea that stimulating the economy at the top of the tax bracket would "trickle down" to the middle and lower classes actually made conditions in the inner cities – where most of the lower class lived – worse.

Between 1980 and 1984, Reagan took away $140 billion from social programs and gave $181 billion to defense. There was a tremendous human cost to these figures. 350,000 people lost Social Security benefits. One Congressional Medal of Honor who had shrapnel in his arms, legs, and chests from the Vietnam War was told that he was not too injured to work. Another man died after he sustained injuries in an oil field accident that both the company doctor and a state supervisor said made him too disabled to work. The government disagreed and forced him back to work. After his death, federal officials said, "We have a p.r. problem."

Yes, the 1980s saw many people get rich, but the problem was that they were already rich. Now they were called "superrich." In 1986, the top tax rate was lowered to 28 percent. This meant that a factory worker, a school teacher, and a billionaire could all pay the same taxes. A billionaire paying the same tax rate as a school teacher is not equitable and can only work to benefit the billionaire.

The S&L disaster is an obvious negative outcome to deregulation, however one that get less notice is the elimination of the FCC's fairness doctrine. American politics have always been bipartisan, meaning that voters tend to align with their parties. However, the rhetoric that has increased due to the emergence of news programs on Fox, MSNBC, and CNN have only served to make the problem worse. It has become increasingly difficult to find a neutral news source and while some may argue that the doctrine increased censorship, it is not a coincidence that "hate radio" has been on the rise over the past two decades. Lack of intelligent discussion over politics has led to baseless arguments where pundits take sides rather than review facts, which can all be traced back to deregulation.

Conclusion

The economics policies that dominated the 1980s were controversial then, as they are now. However, if Americans were surprised by the policies and actions of President Ronald Reagan, they should not have been. Governor Reagan gave a glimpse into what was to come should he be elected to a higher office. When he assumed office in 1967, California had a significant budget deficit. Reagan's response was to institute a 10 percent decrease in spending by the state, only to have to give some of the money back because he had cut some programs so far, they couldn't function.

Governor Reagan signed the largest tax increase in California history because the state needed the money. By the time he left office in 1975, he had spent twice as much as the previous governor, Pat Brown. Governor Reagan also talked about reducing government, but in many ways, it grew. This had a familiar ring to it when Reagan concluded his presidency.

Debating about political performance is a challenge because people often debate with their hearts – or their political affiliation – more than their heads. Facts are often obscured by feelings and soundbites from radio or television broadcasts. And, when Reagan first left the White House, the analysis of Reaganomics was not, in general, favorable. This could be due to the Iran – Contra Affair, which is not part of the discussion of Reaganomics, but is definitely part of the discussion about Reagan.

Reagan grew to be called "The Teflon President." Like a Teflon-coated frying pan, it seemed that nothing "stuck" to him. No scandal seemed to impact his popularity. Congresswoman Pat Schroeder from Colorado first gave Reagan the nickname and she said it fit because of one of his other nicknames, The Great Communicator. Reagan's public speaking abilities are undeniable and he could explain – or explain away anything. When it was discovered that the U.S. government had a secret arrangement to give money to rebels in Nicaragua in from profits for selling guns to Iran, he said he didn't know about it. Reagan was far enough removed from day-to-day activities at the White House, an arrangement that was initially enforced while he was recovering from his gunshot wound and stuck for eight more years, that it was plausible he didn't know.

Whether he did or didn't know, it didn't impact his popularity with the public, but it may have impacted the so-called experts when they tallied up the pros and cons of Reagan's policies. It seems as if it should be easy to rank a president's performance. After all, numbers don't lie. Or do they? Saying Reaganomics resulted in more jobs does not tell the whole picture about what *kind* of jobs he created. Pointing out that Reagan's support of raised interest rates in his first term led to a recession does not explain what happened *after* the recession ended.

Consulting polls and surveys to help rank the performance of Reaganomics does not help. Depending on what poll you consult, Reagan is ranked anywhere from 6th all the way down to 34th of all president's in American history. So, what is the truth? The truth is somewhere in between 6th and 34th.

Generally speaking, the wealthy – or at least the well off – rank Reagan highly and are a fan of his policies. The wealthy are usually involved in business ventures and Reaganomics was a friend to business. It is hard to argue that the economy in the 1980s did experience a boom after inflation was tamed. Often called "The Great Expansion," the period beginning in 1982 and continued into the 1990s was a time of unprecedented growth. The economy grew for a record 92 months in a row before hitting a brief recession in 1990 and 1991. Economist Lawrence B. Lindsay and former governor of the Federal Reserve said, "The years after 1983 are best viewed as a single expansion, with its roots in the policy changes in the late 1970s and early 1980s." While Reagan is not responsible for all of the growth into the 90s, he certainly is responsible for some of it.

However, many poor people, or simply those that struggled do not remember Reagan fondly. There is no evidence at all that Reagan tried to run up a deficit to make it impossible to fund social programs. It seems more likely he just wanted to the threat of a deficit out there and got more than be bargained for. Nonetheless, Reagan will be remembered by very few as sensitive to the needs of those near the bottom of the socioeconomic bracket. Even his lifestyle as a former actor who still liked to tell old Hollywood stories and had friends in the entertainment industry worked to separate him from the masses. He seemed out of touch with societal ills. The drug problem was combatted by First Lady Nancy Reagan's "Just Say No" campaign and he virtually ignored another scourge of the 80s, AIDS, until an old Hollywood friend, Rock Hudson developed the disease and died.

Whatever the assessment on Reaganomics is, he is remembered as an optimist. He came along at a time when voters wanted to believe in America again and were having doubts that America was, indeed, exceptional. He refueled a sense of patriotism and even if he was not responsible for ending the Cold War, his staunch hatred for Communism was no act and American loved him for standing up to the Soviets.

Right or wrong, for better or for worse, Reaganomics was implemented because Reagan touched a nerve with America and they trusted him. It is a sad irony that a man whose presidency was so steeped in his ability to communicate lost that ability late in life due to Alzheimer's disease. He was not smooth, like a used car salesman. He was genuine, like a grandfather. There is room for both blame and celebration in his policies. However, the story of Reaganomics cannot be told and grasped without an understanding of Reagan himself. His ability to persuade Americans to buy into his optimism and trust in his policies, often phrased using words that Americans wanted to hear, were as much a part of Reaganomics as the statistics.

Made in the USA
Lexington, KY
18 February 2013